forever mom

forever mom

inspiring words on motherhood

edited by anne howard

Published in North America in 2006
by Tangent Publications
an imprint of
Axis Publishing Limited
8c Accommodation Road
London NW11 8ED
www.axispublishing.co.uk

Creative Director: Siân Keogh
Editorial Director: Anne Yelland
Production Manager: Jo Ryan
Production Controller: Cécile Lerbiere

ISBN 1-904707-29-7

2 4 6 8 10 9 7 5 3 1

Printed and bound in China

about this book

Written by and for moms and their children of all ages, this collection of witty,

thought-provoking, and life-affirming sayings and quotations offers a refreshing

take on the joys and trials of being a mother. Generations of moms and kids

offer their words of wisdom on this special relationship. These are the words of

real moms, and their sons and daughters, designed to offer to your mother, and

to friends who are new moms or moms-to-be. The sayings are complemented

by a series of amusing animal photographs, guaranteed to inspire and enthrall.

This is an ideal gift book for mothers and moms-to-be, and an inspirational

reminder of this special relationship.

about the author

Anne Howard is an experienced writer and editor with many years' publishing experience, who specializes in books on pregnancy and childcare. From the many hundreds of thoughts that were sent to her by people from all over the world, she has selected those with the broadest appeal to fill this collection.

A mother understands
what a child does not say.

A mother's love enables her child to achieve the impossible.

Motherhood is the most beautiful of all the arts.

A mother gives you life
but cannot live it for you.

Love begins and ends
with motherhood.

A mother's arms are made of tenderness, and children sleep sound within them.

The best medicine in the world
is a mother's kiss.

Motherhood is a
wonderful thing.

Mother is the bank where we deposit all our hurts and worries.

A mother makes a home.

There is no substitute for a mother.

A mother loves her children, especially when they least deserve it.

A mother's love is unconditional.

The joys of motherhood are never truly experienced until the children are in bed.

A mother can give you love,
but she can't force it on you.

Mother is home.

Men are what their
mothers make them.

There is a mother at the
beginning of all great things.

A man loves his sweetheart the most, his wife the best, but his mother the longest.

Moms can do anything.

All that I am I owe
to my mother.

When it comes to love,
mom's the word.

A mother's heart is
a child's schoolroom.

Children are the anchors that
hold a mother to life.

A mother's love enables
a child to do anything.

A mother's dignity comes from being unknown to the world and her pleasure lies in the happiness of her family.

A mother's children are
portraits of herself.

The hand that rocks the cradle
belongs to someone who is
not getting enough sleep.

No gift to your mother can
ever equal her gift to you…

…life.

Without good mothers,
civilization is doomed.

A mother's love
endures through all.

A mother who is really
a mother is never free.

A mother's voice is always soft, gentle, and low.

A mother is the truest friend.

A mother is an angel
from God.

A joyful mother makes
happy children.

A mother's love is mighty.

The first home was made when a woman, cradling her baby in her arms, sang a lullaby.

All love begins and
ends with motherhood.

Stories first heard at a mother's knee are never forgotten.

The heart of a mother is
a deep abyss at the
bottom of which you will
always find forgiveness.

A mother's love is peace.

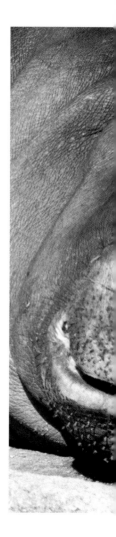

Children live what they learn from their mothers.

Motherhood is the
most important of all
the professions.

A mother's love is never unsure.

What is a home
without a mother?

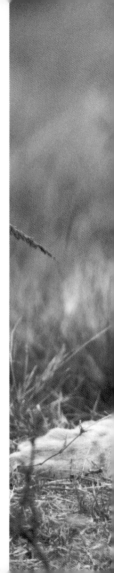

There's no substitute
for a mother.

All that I am and can ever
hope to be I owe to my mother.

To the world a mother is one person, but to her child she is the world.

If I had a flower for every time I thought of my mother, I could walk in my garden for ever.

There is no rose
so beautiful as a
mother's smile.

A mother's love never
fails or falters.

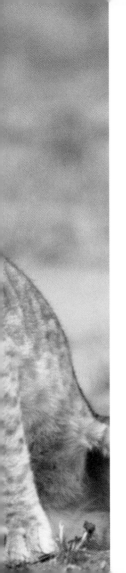

To a child's ear, mother is magic in any language.

A mother's heart is always
with her children.

Children are the sum of what mothers contribute to their lives.

A child reminds us that playtime is an essential part of our daily routine.

In their children mothers
give birth to the future.

A mother is the truest
friend we have.

A mother is a child's constant teacher and companion.

There is no velvet as
soft as a mother's lap.